how to have fun weaving

By Editors of Creative

Illustrated by Betty Sievert

DEDICATED TO
TOM, MIKE, KRISTY and TIMMY

creative
craft
book

Library of Congress Number: 73-12467
ISBN: 0-87191-272-4

Published by Creative Education, Mankato, Minnesota 56001. Distributed by Childrens Press, 1224 West Van Buren Street, Chicago, Illinois 60607

Library of Congress Cataloging in Publication Data
Creative Educational Society, Mankato, Minn.
    How to have fun weaving.
            (Creative craft books)
    SUMMARY: A brief history of weaving, instructions for basic weaving steps and making a loom, and directions for three simple projects.
    1. Hand weaving—Juvenile literature. [1. Hand weaving. 2. Handicraft] I. Title.
TT848.C65 746.1'4 73-12467
ISBN 0-87191-272-4

ABOUT WEAVING

Weaving is a very old craft. In the New Stone Age cavemen used straw and reeds to make baskets as well as threads from the flax plant to make clothing. They learned that it was much harder to weave threads from the flax plant and that they needed something to guide the threads. The frame on which they placed the threads to guide them is called a loom. The first cloth made on the looms was very rough. But, by the time of the ancient Egyptians, linen weaving was a fine art.

In about 2000 B.C. the threads of silkworm cocoons were being unwound by the Chinese and they were weaving them into cloth. And, the people of India discovered how to make cloth from the cotton plant.

In the Middle Ages and Renaissance women would weave cloth in their own homes by using crude hand made looms. They would then make the clothing for all of the members of the family.

Mats and rugs for the floors of the settlers homes in early America were made at home by the women. But hand weaving almost became a lost art in America.

As weaving changed from a craft to an art, looms were made bigger and more involved. Weaving changed from a necessary household duty to a modern mechanized industry. The principles of weaving have not changed. It is the looms that have changed.

Today our fabrics are woven in large mills. The entire weaving process is performed by machines. Few human workers are required to handle these looms. Already looms are producing cloth made entirely from synthetic materials. But it remains a popular craft today for very skillful artists that weave our very beautiful rugs and the tapestries used for wall hangings and furniture coverings. And, weaving is now a creative art.

LET'S BEGIN

You can enjoy this ancient craft. From a single square you can get a pot holder — or by sewing several squares together you can get a placemat. Once you know the basic weaving steps you will be able to create many projects that you can use for gifts. The only materials you need to enjoy this craft are yarn and a loom.

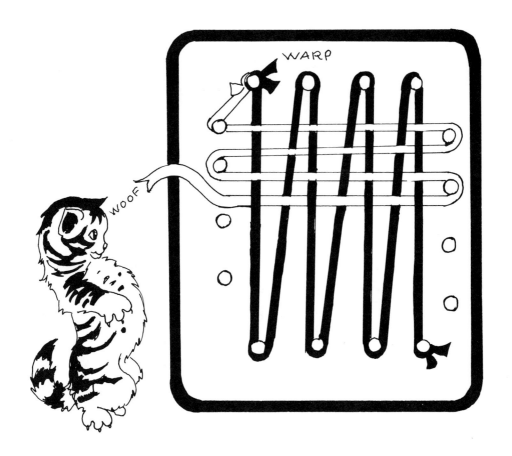

The thread or yarn that you use for your first project should be easy for you to work with. Try to find some heavy wool yarn, rug yarn, colored cord or plastic cord to begin on. You can even use textured rope.

A word that you will need to know is warp. The warp is the set of threads that you will put lengthwise on your loom. The warp threads are then crossed for weaving.

Let's Begin with the basic weaving steps. Once you know these basic steps you will be able to create many of your own patterns.

The three basic weaving steps are plain weave, the satin weave and the twill weave.

For the PLAIN WEAVE lengthwise threads (warp) are evenly placed on the loom. The crosswise threads go over one thread, under the next, over the next. This is continued until the material is woven. The Plain weave is the tightest and most common of basic weave steps. It makes a checkered pattern. Some cloths made from plain weaving are gingham, percale, linen, woolen, and tweeds.

The TWILL WEAVE is made by crossing the lengthwise threads with the crosswise threads unevenly. They are woven over and under two or more warp threads. The finished cloth has rows of diagonally raised lines. Since the threads are drawn very tightly, cloth made from the twill weave will give longer wear. Two cloths made with this weave are gabardines and twills.

For the SATIN WEAVE the cross threads cross the warp at widely spaced intervals.

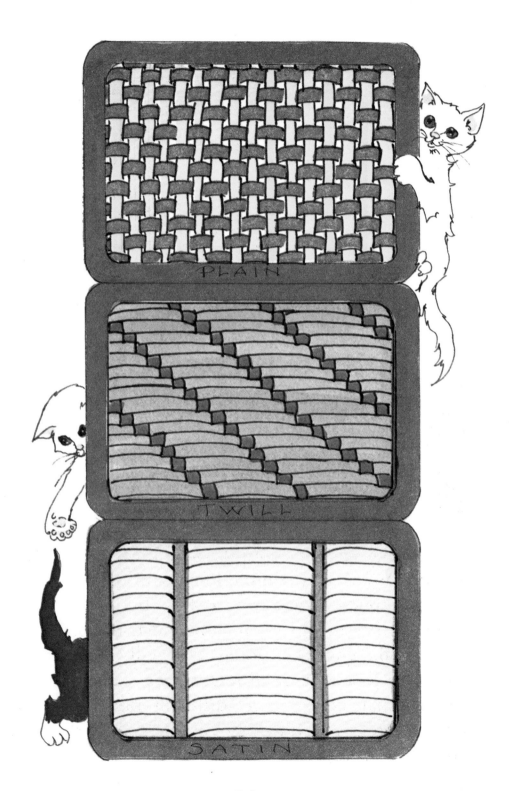

PLAIN

TWILL

SATIN

11

FRAME LOOM

MAKING A LOOM

Looms are very simple and can be made from many, many things. Simple looms can be made from picture frames. You can also buy Inkle and frame looms. You can buy looms on which to weave but if you make your own looms you will find that you can make looms many different sizes. Then you will be able to make as many different projects as you want. Here are a few very simple looms that you can make at home.

CARDBOARD

WOOD

WOOD

CARDBOARD

13

A Cardboard Loom

Find a piece of stiff cardboard. You can use very heavy poster board, a piece from a box or any other heavy piece you are able to find around the house. Make the cardboard a little larger than the size you want your finished project to be.

To make tabs on your loom, use a ruler and mark off every ¼ inch. Make a border ½″ inside the edge of the cardboard. Draw your border all around the cardboard. Now cut out each notch with a scissors. Cut each notch in a triangle up to your border.

Now your loom is ready for you to place your warp threads on. You will start the warp threads at one edge. Wind it completely around the cardboard and into the next notch. Continue until you have all of the warp threads on your loom.

Then you can begin weaving.

A Wooden Loom

All you need is a board. On the board you can pound nails in the design that you want. It can be a square, circle, or any other interesting shape that you can design yourself. Draw your design on the board first. Make it a little larger than you want your finished project. Always be sure that each nail is spaced the same distance as the other nails.

EASY WEAVING PROJECTS

We are going to begin with some very simple weaving projects. You will be able to make many interesting and useful gifts from these very simple projects. After you have completed these projects try to weave in different patterns.

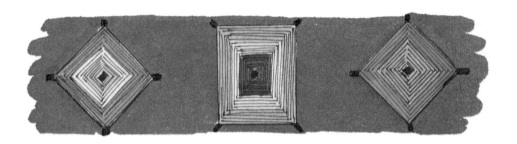

A Wall Hanging

The Hopi Indians used a very simple method of weaving to make "Good Luck Charms". For this project you will need 2 sticks that are 12 inches long. You could even use two pieces of wire from a clothes hanger. Take the two sticks and lay one lengthwise and one crosswise. Where the two sticks meet in the middle attach them with a rubber band, wire or glue.

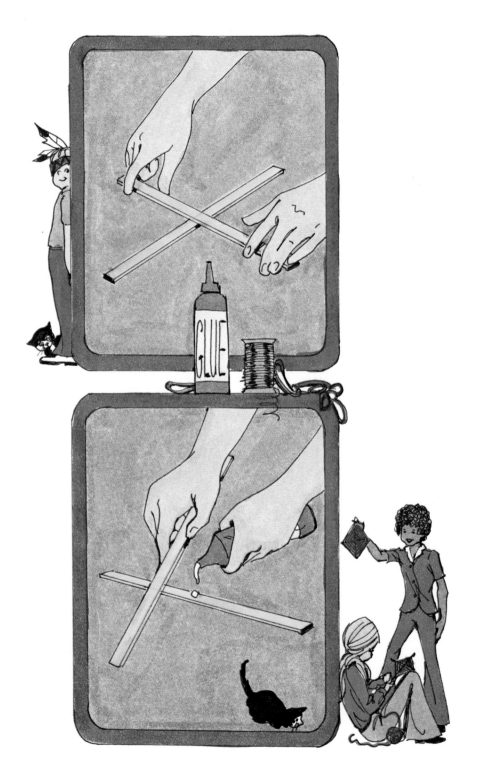

Now, take some yarn, embroidery thread, string or whatever you have decided to weave with, and wrap it around one of the wires. Tie it in a knot. Continue to the next wire. Wrap it over, under and back over to the next wire. You can do this on all of the wires. Always go the same way. If you want to change the color of your thread, just tie the other color on and keep weaving. When you finish make sure all knots are pulled to the back side so that they will not show.

When you are ready to finish, wrap the last thread around the wire you want to end on. Wrap it around several times and then tie it in a knot. Cut end.

You are now ready to hang your wall hanging. These are very fast to make so that you could make them different colors for presents.

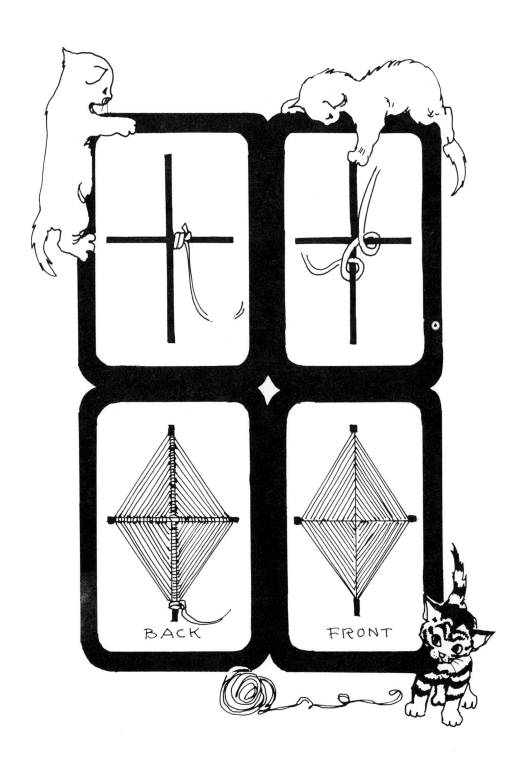

BACK   FRONT

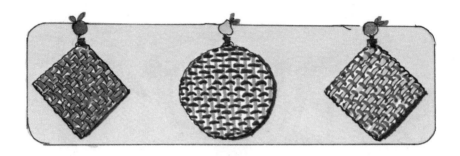

Potholders

A potholder is very easy to make. It does not take much yarn. And, it does not take long to complete. We are going to make square potholders. They are much easier to make than round ones. Once you have finished weaving several square potholders try making a round one. But, make your round potholders on a wooden loom.

Make a 4½ inch square cardboard loom. You begin your potholder by putting on your warp threads. Start at the top of the loom and warp your yarn from the top notch to the bottom one. Go around the back side and bring the yarn up to the next notch. Continue until all notches are done. Then, begin by weaving in and out (up and under) with your cross thread. It will be very easy for you to do this if you use a needle for your thread or yarn. Do not put too much yarn on so that it is difficult for you to work with and becomes tangled. Leave about two inches of yarn at the beginning of your cross threads.

Do not weave on both sides of the loom. Leave the warp threads on the back side empty. When you come to the end of the first row, you will finish by staying in your pattern of weaving in and out on the last warp thread in that row. Then bring it down to the second row. Do not pull the cross threads too tight. On the second row continue to weave in and out. Do this so that the threads on the first row you did in will be out on the second row. Push each row down so that it will be tight on the loom. Continue weaving all of the rows until you are at the end of your loom. Whenever you want to change the color of your thread, just tie the new color on and continue weaving. When you are at the end of your loom very carefully remove the warp threads from your loom.

Now, finish your potholder by cutting the warp threads that were on the back of your loom. Cut these in the middle of the loom. Tie two ends together all the way across the top and bottom. Clip the ends.

From this simple little square potholder you can make many other interesting projects. If you make six of these potholders and sew them together, you have a placemat. Then, you might even want to leave the fringe on one side of four of the squares. Or, if want to make 36 squares, you could sew them together and make a scarf. Again, you might want to leave the fringe on the end squares.

Placemats

Placemats can be made many ways. Let's make one that is all in one piece. This can easily be done in an afternoon. Why not make enough for your family.

We are going to use a wooden loom. All you need is a large board. Draw a square on your board that is 11 inches wide and 16 inches long. Now, using a ruler at the top of your square, mark off every ¼ inch. Mark off the bottom in the same way. Now, pound your nails in, just a little ways, on the ¼ inch markings.

Thread your warp threads by going back and forth across the nails on the loom. From the top nail to the one on the bottom. To hold the first one on the nail, tie a knot. Also tie a knot at the last nail. Once you have all the warp threads on you are ready to begin weaving.

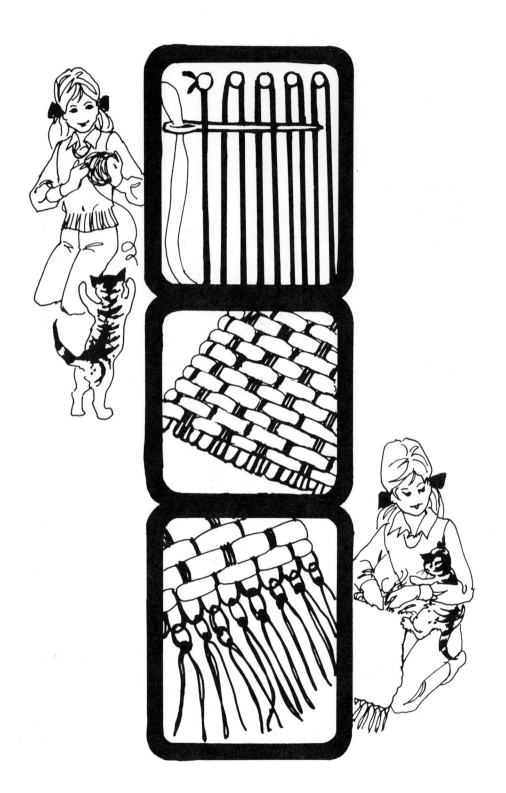

Let's do this in a pattern that is very fast. Put your yarn on a needle. Under one thread, over three. On the second row do under three, over one. Push each row down tightly against the last row. Continue this pattern until you are at the bottom.

Remove your placemat from the loom very carefully. Now take small strands of your thread and put through each loop. Tie in a knot. Now cut your fringe so that it will be even. Tie any loose ends. Make sure all knots from thread changes are pulled to the back side.

This same pattern and board can be used to make smaller or larger projects.

Someday when you want a real project, find a very large board and make a rug in this same way. Remember that you can also make different shapes on your board. Once you have completed all of these projects, go back and try making them in different weaving steps. They will look completely different. Or, change weaving steps on the same project and have several patterns. You will be able to create many different gifts by just using your own ideas.

how to have fun

creative
craft
books